I0828190

THIS BOOK BELONGS TO:

WELCOME TO NEW JERSEY

Dedicated to all the explorers.

All rights reserved.
No part of this book may be reproduced in any form or by any means, electronic or mechanical, and no photocopying or recording, unless you have written permission from the author.

ISBN 978-1-970416-00-8

Text copyright © 2026 by Mimi Jones

www.joeysavestheday.com

Mimi Books™ Publishing
© 2021–Present Mimi Books

A Mimi Book

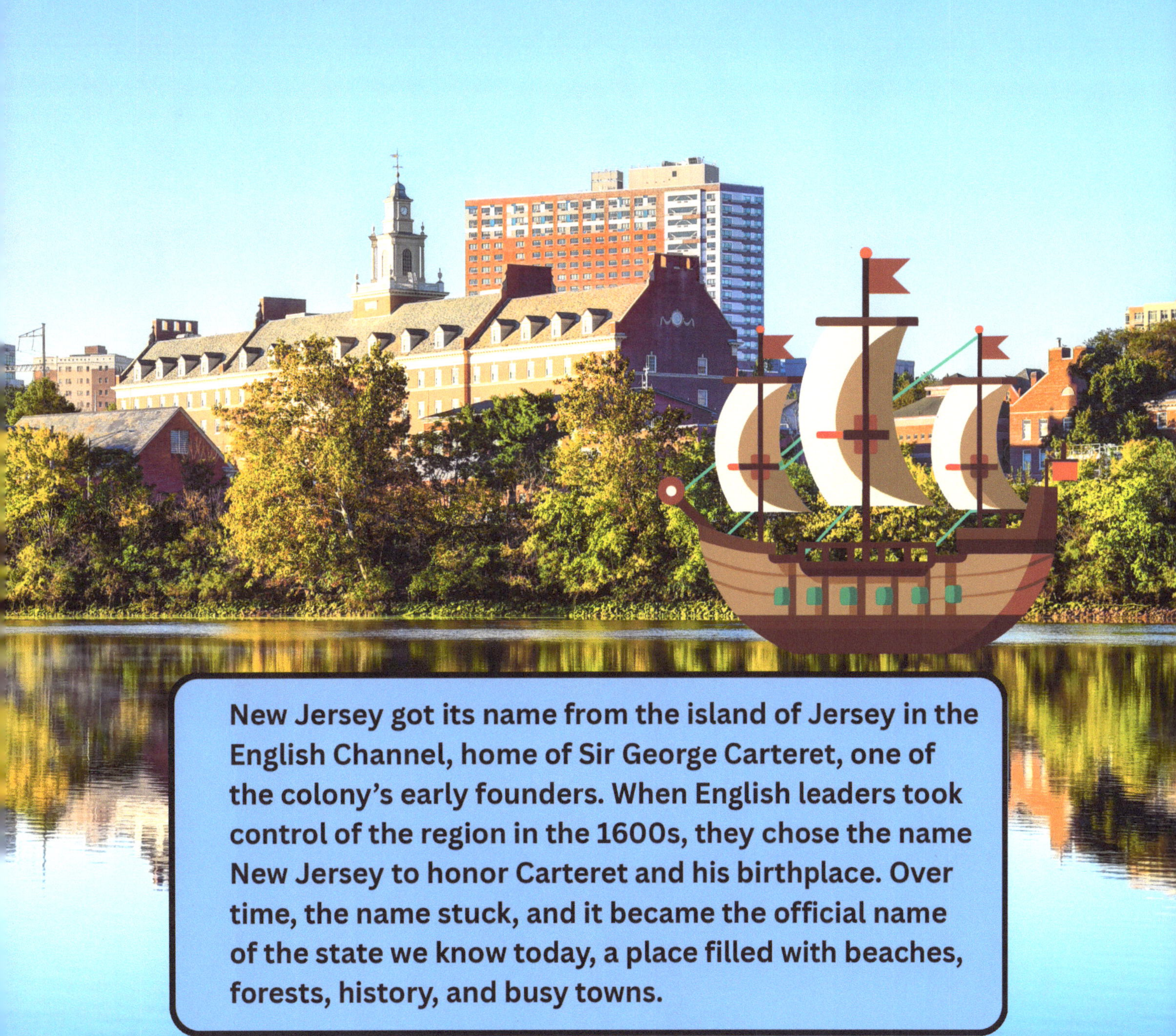

New Jersey got its name from the island of Jersey in the English Channel, home of Sir George Carteret, one of the colony's early founders. When English leaders took control of the region in the 1600s, they chose the name New Jersey to honor Carteret and his birthplace. Over time, the name stuck, and it became the official name of the state we know today, a place filled with beaches, forests, history, and busy towns.

New Jersey's history begins with Native American groups such as the Lenape, who lived in the region for thousands of years, fishing, farming, and building villages along the rivers and coast. In the 1600s, Dutch and Swedish settlers arrived, followed later by the English, who took control and named the area New Jersey. Because of its location between major colonies, New Jersey became an important crossroads during the American Revolution, with many key battles fought on its land.

New Jersey was the third state to join the Union. It officially joined on December 18, 1787.

New Jersey is located in the Mid-Atlantic region of the United States. It is bordered by New York to the north and east, Pennsylvania to the west, and Delaware to the southwest, with long stretches of coastline along the Atlantic Ocean.

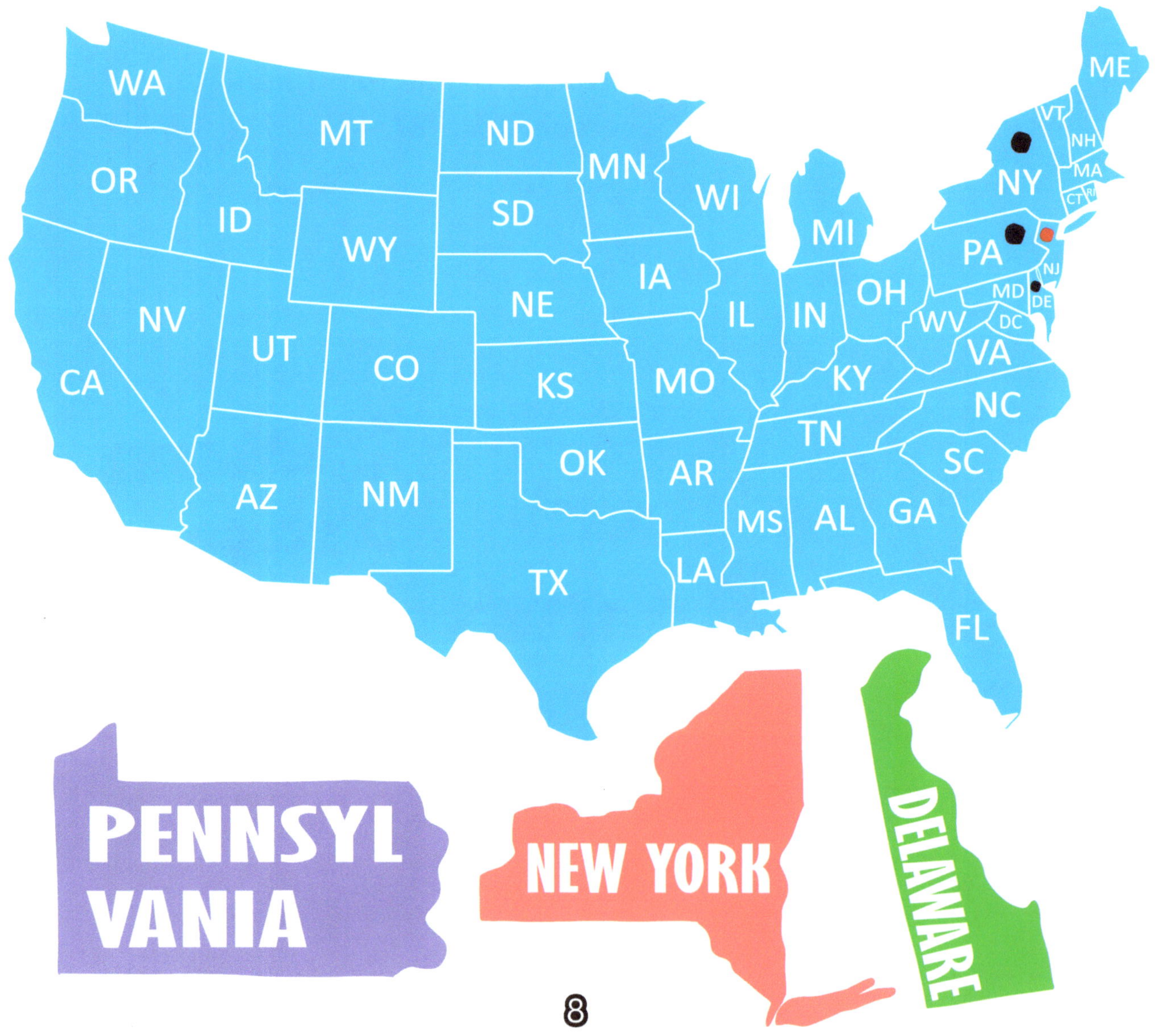

Trenton is the capital of New Jersey.
It officially became the capital in 1790.

Trenton, New Jersey, has an estimated population of about 91,000.

New Jersey is the forty-seventh largest state in the United States by area.

47th

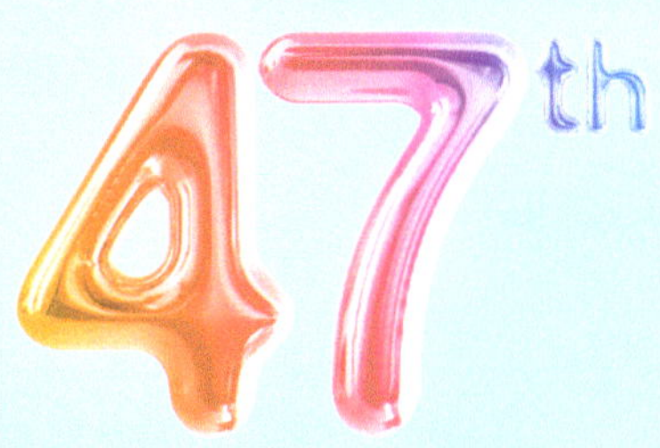

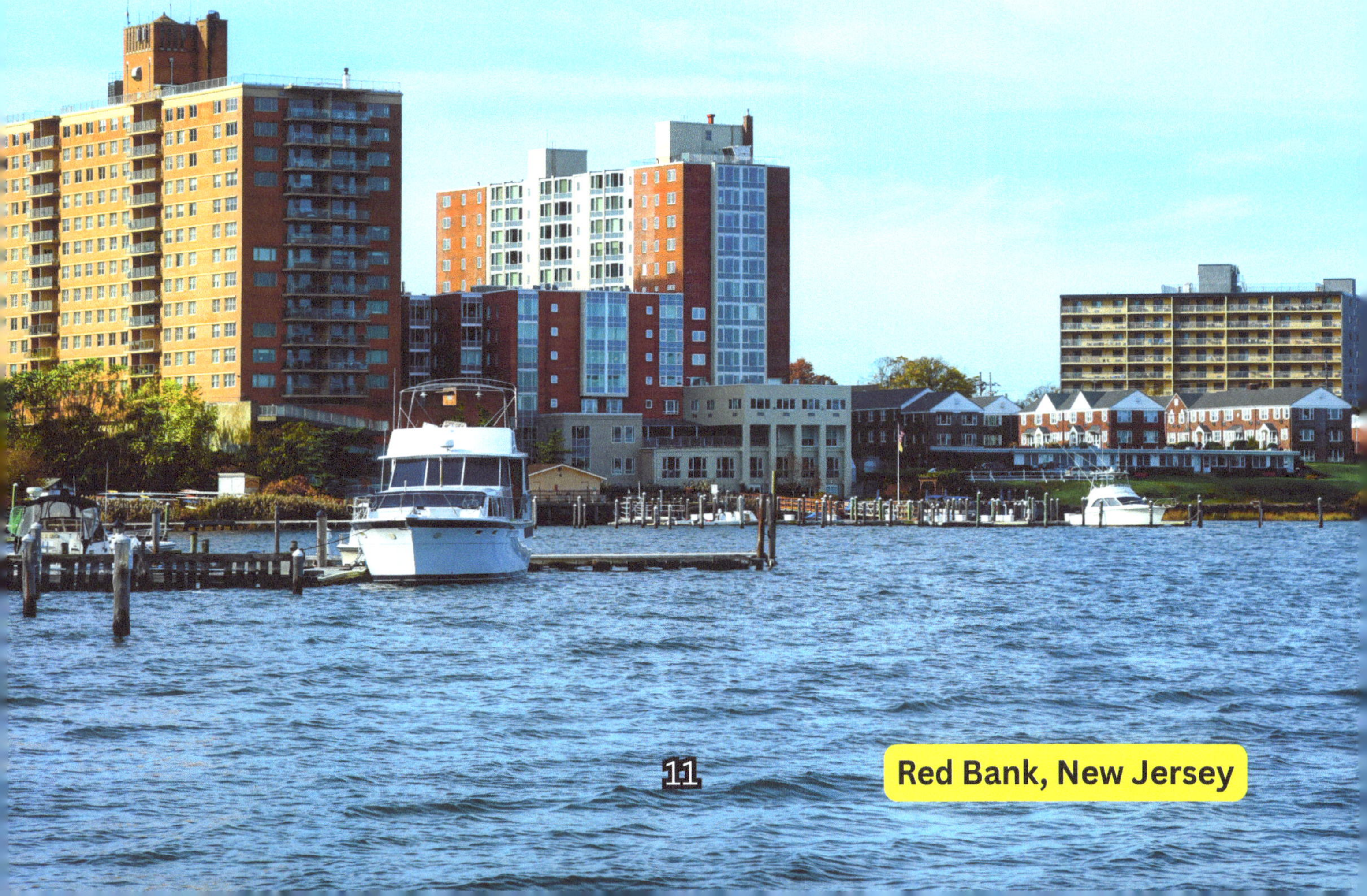

Red Bank, New Jersey

There are approximately 9,550,000 people residing in the state of New Jersey.

Thomas Edison, one of America's greatest inventors, is remembered at the Thomas Edison National Historical Park in West Orange, New Jersey. His old brick laboratory buildings still stand, filled with tools, machines, and inventions that helped change the world. Inside the museum, visitors can see Edison's original workspaces where he created things like the phonograph and improved electric light bulbs. It's a special place where families can explore how curiosity, creativity, and hard work helped shape modern life.

New Jersey is famous for its sweet saltwater taffy! This chewy, colorful candy was first made on the Atlantic City Boardwalk more than 100 years ago. Kids and families love picking their favorite flavors, from strawberry to chocolate to classic vanilla. Saltwater taffy has become one of New Jersey's happiest seaside traditions and a favorite treat for visitors all summer long.

TRADITION

NEW JERSEY

There are 21 counties in New Jersey.

Here is a list of twenty of those counties:

Atlantic	Cumberland	Mercer	Passaic
Bergen	Essex	Middlesex	Salem
Burlington	Gloucester	Monmouth	Somerset
Camden	Hudson	Morris	Sussex
Cape May	Hunterdon	Ocean	Warren

Paterson Great Falls is one of New Jersey's most powerful natural landmarks, with water rushing over a tall basalt cliff into the Passaic River below. The falls were shaped by ancient lava flows and thousands of years of moving water, creating the deep, rocky gorge that surrounds them today.

Paterson Great Falls National Historical Park

One of the most important moments in New Jersey's history is George Washington's famous crossing of the Delaware River in 1776. On a freezing winter night, the Continental Army traveled from Pennsylvania into New Jersey to launch a surprise attack that boosted hope during the Revolutionary War. Their victory encouraged more people to support independence and helped keep the army strong. Today, Washington Crossing State Park marks the spot, reminding visitors how this brave event helped shape America's future.

The Bayonne Bridge

The Bayonne Bridge is a historic landmark that connects Bayonne, New Jersey, to Staten Island, New York, high above the busy Kill Van Kull waterway. Opened in 1931, this massive steel arch bridge was once the longest of its kind in the world, making it a huge engineering achievement for its time.

The New Jersey state bird is the Eastern Goldfinch. It was chosen as the state bird in 1935.

The official state flower of New Jersey is the Violet. It was chosen as the state flower in 1971.

A couple of New Jersey's nicknames include the Garden State and the Crossroads of the Revolution.

ST8

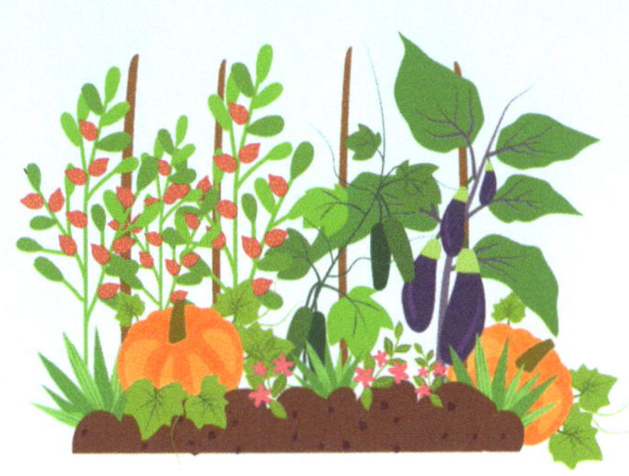

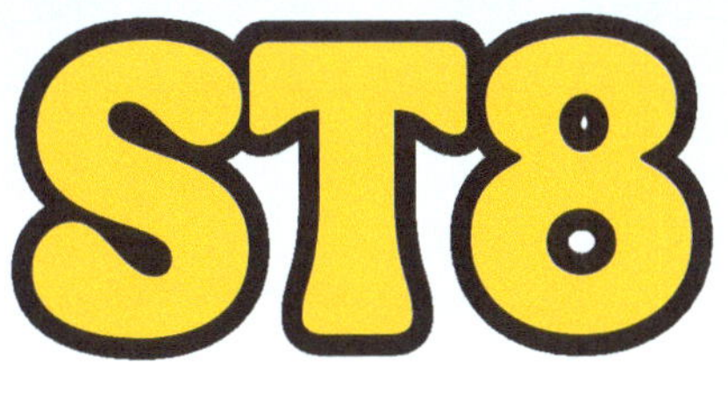

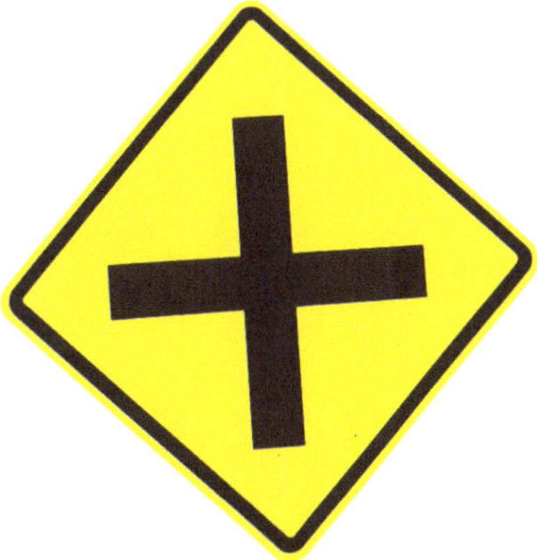

of THE REVOLUTION

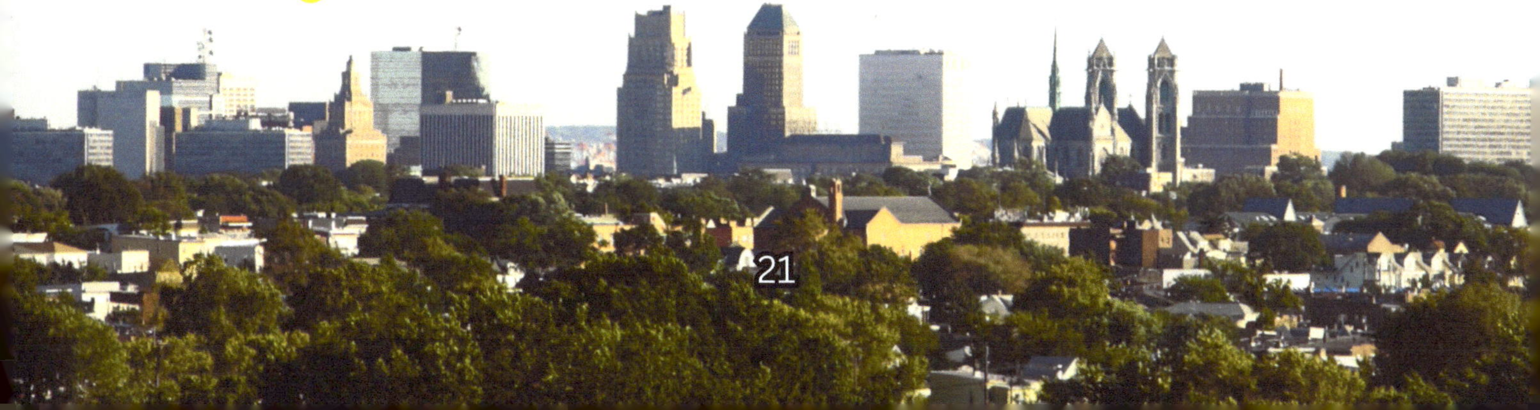

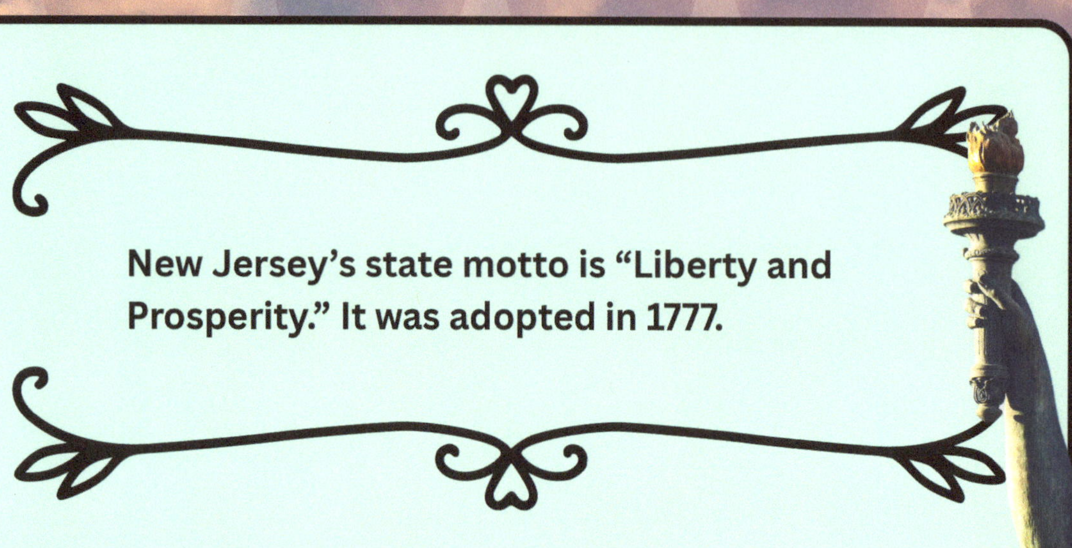

New Jersey's state motto is "Liberty and Prosperity." It was adopted in 1777.

What "Liberty and Prosperity" Means:

- Liberty means people have the freedom to make choices, share their ideas, and live their lives without unfair control.
- Prosperity means having the chance to grow, succeed, and build a good life through hard work and opportunity.

Put together, the motto is saying:
New Jersey believes in protecting people's freedoms while helping communities grow strong and successful.

The abbreviation for New Jersey is NJ.

NJ

New Jersey's state flag was officially adopted in 1896.

Some crops grown in New Jersey are blueberries, bell peppers, peaches, cranberries, and spinach.

Some animals that live in New Jersey are white-tailed deer, red foxes, black bears, river otters, and great horned owls.

New Jersey experiences a wide range of temperatures throughout the year. The hottest temperature ever recorded in the state was 110 degrees Fahrenheit, measured in Runyon on July 10, 1936. In contrast, the coldest temperature documented was –34 degrees Fahrenheit, recorded in River Vale on January 5, 1904.

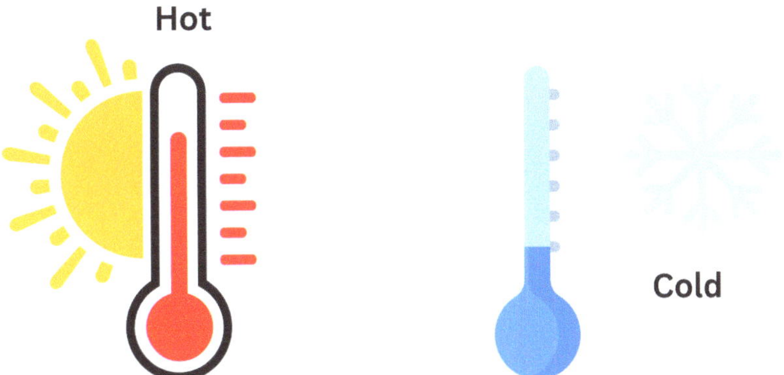

The Cape May County Park & Zoo in southern New Jersey is a wonderful place to explore, with animals from all around the world. Kids can see lions, giraffes, zebras, snow leopards, and playful primates, along with colorful birds and reptiles.

Buzz Aldrin was a brave astronaut from New Jersey who helped make history. He was one of the first two people to walk on the Moon during the Apollo 11 mission in 1969. Kids remember him for his courage, his love of exploration, and his important role in one of America's greatest space achievements.

The largest airport in New Jersey is Newark Liberty International Airport, located in Newark and Elizabeth. It sits at 3 Brewster Road and serves as the main travel hub for people flying in and out of New Jersey. This airport connects travelers to cities all across the country and to destinations around the world, making it one of the busiest and most important airports on the East Coast.

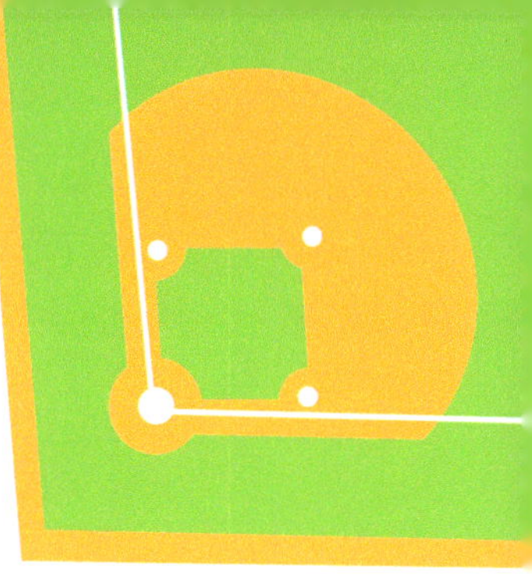

The Somerset Patriots are a professional baseball team from New Jersey, and many families across the state love cheering for them. They play their home games at TD Bank Ballpark, a bright and welcoming stadium known for its fun atmosphere, friendly fans, and exciting summer nights. The Patriots are part of Minor League Baseball and help develop talented players as they work toward the major leagues.

FOOTBALL

The New York Giants are a major professional football team with a huge fan base all across New Jersey, where many families cheer for them every season. The team plays its home games at MetLife Stadium in East Rutherford, a loud and exciting stadium filled with fans wearing blue, red, and white.

The red oak is New Jersey's state tree. It's known for its wide, sturdy branches and deep green leaves that turn bright shades of red in the fall. The red oak was officially adopted as the state tree in 1950, and its strong wood and beautiful autumn colors have made it a proud symbol of New Jersey's natural beauty.

The brook trout is New Jersey's state fish. It's a small, colorful fish with bright spots and a shimmering pattern that make it easy to recognize in cool, clear streams. The brook trout was officially adopted as the state fish in 1991, and its beauty and connection to New Jersey's clean, flowing waters make it a beloved symbol of the state's natural habitats.

Can you name these?

I hope you enjoyed learning about New Jersey.

To explore fun facts about the other 49 states, visit my website at www.joeysavestheday.com. You'll also find a wide variety of homeschool resources to support joyful learning at home. If you enjoyed this book, I would be grateful if you left a review. Your feedback truly helps. Thank you for your support!

Check out these other interesting books in the 50 States Fact Books Series!

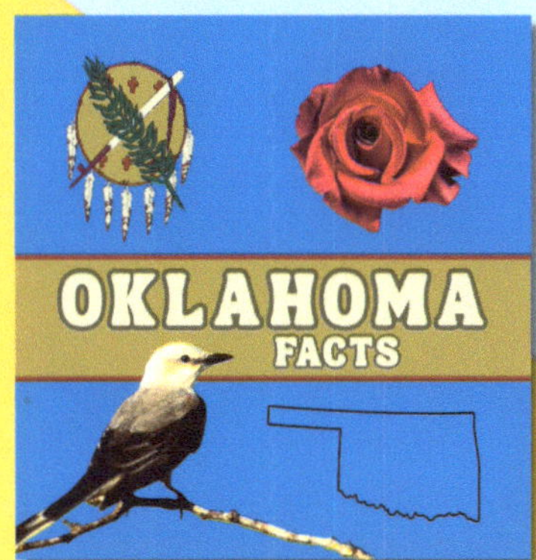

www.ingramcontent.com/pod-product-compliance
Lightning Source LLC
LaVergne TN
LVHW070201110826
845147LV00002B/462
9781970416008